Introduction

No matter where you live, your favorite fabric store is overflowing with an array of colorful and practical polyester fleece. This fabric is made soft the same way corduroy and velvet are—by brushing the surface fibers with plastic bristles and then cutting them with a spiral blade. But unlike corduroy and velvet, fleece has a two-sided pile. The double-sided pile is doubly good because both sides are nice and fuzzy, giving fleece the warmth of wool without the heft. Because of its lofty texture and exceptional warmth, it has become a popular choice for crafters everywhere.

The fabric store experience is tactile and visual, and that's especially true in the fleece section. But what can you make with this delightful material beyond the common knotted blanket? After years of experimenting and exploring we have fashioned 30 easy designs that will take you beyond the land of clunky knots and into dreamy downy heaven. Enjoy the ride … and you're welcome!

Trice

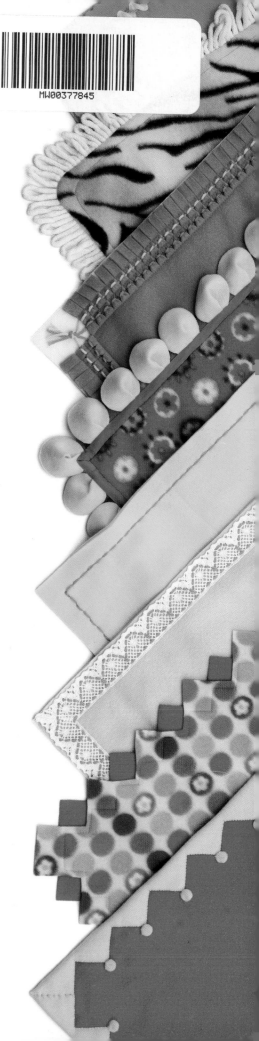

Meet the Designer

Trice Boerens has worked for many years in the quilting, needlework and paper industries. Along with designing projects for best-selling books and kits, she has also worked as a photo stylist, an art director and a creative editor.

She loves working with fleece because it is soft and fuzzy, does not ravel and comes in an array of colors and patterns.

Table of Contents

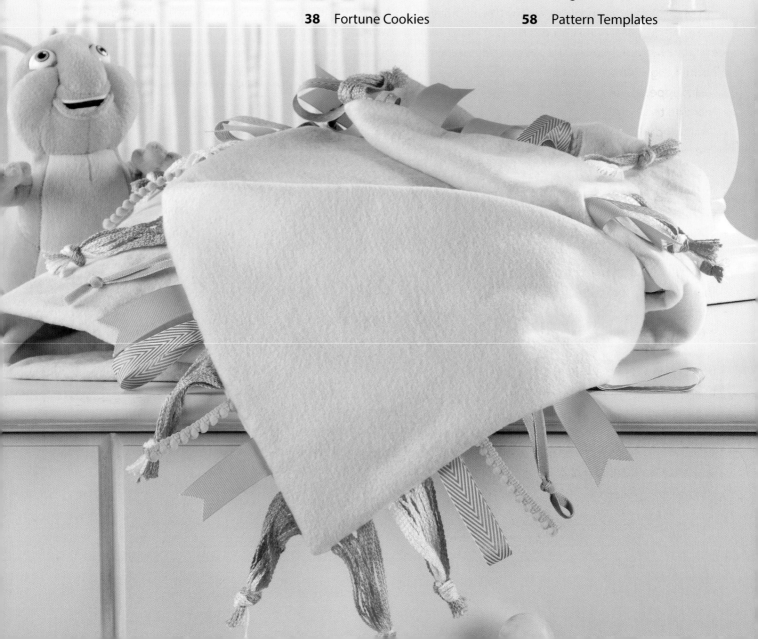

General Instructions

If you are a beginner to sewing with fleece, this section will help you gather the basic supplies and tools you need. The hints provided will guarantee a successful sewing experience.

Basic Sewing Supplies & Equipment

- Sewing machine and ballpoint or Microtex needles
- Coordinating or contrasting polyester thread
- Hand-sewing needles, including tapestry needles
- Long straight pins
- Seam ripper
- Marking tool
- Straightedge
- Tracing paper, pencil and scissors reserved for cutting paper
- Rotary cutter, specialty blades, self-healing mat and clear straightedge ruler
- Shears reserved for cutting cloth: Paper will dull blades quickly. Never use your sewing shears, scissors or rotary cutter to cut anything other than fabric.
- Turning tool (optional): A turning tool is a rod or a tube with a blunt end that is used to push the fabric into the corner to make a right angle. If you don't have a tool made specifically for turning, use a knitting needle with a rounded end, or use the eraser end of a pencil.
- Template material: This is a transparent material onto which the provided patterns can be traced. Then use the template to transfer designs to the fleece top or applied shapes.

Sewing With Polyester Fleece

Keep a vacuum cleaner close by when cutting and working with fleece.

Use ballpoint or Microtex needles to avoid skipped stitches. We recommend size 90/14 or size 80/12.

Increase stitch length to 3–3.5mm.

Use long, sharp pins to secure layers. Never stitch over pins. If you strike a pin or pinhead with your sewing machine needle, you will damage the needle, the pin and possibly the sewing machine.

Use quality polyester thread.

Cut blanket tops and bottoms along the grain line. If the fleece nap hides the grain line, cut parallel to the bound or selvage edge.

Fleece does have a right and wrong side, although it is hard to tell by looking at it. Pull the fleece across the cross-grain edge, and it will curl toward the wrong side. Fleece will not fray, which has advantages when making blankets—edges and seams do not have to be finished.

Fleece has a tendency to stretch, so be especially careful not to pull on edges when stitching.

Moving parts of the sewing machine tend to chew up the fabric if you stitch too closely to the cut edge. Use at least a ½-inch seam allowance when joining layers. Trim seam allowance after stitching if necessary. When using the sewing machine for machine appliqué, sew ¼ inch from the edge of the cut shape. If necessary, use the pointed end of a seam ripper to carefully feed the edge under the presser foot.

Experiment with tension, stitch length and speed on a scrap of fleece. Longer stitches are recommended. Since one layer of fleece is bulky, two layers are even bulkier. When joining two layers, grasp the edges next to the lowered presser foot and pull slightly to begin the seam.

An even-feed or walking foot may be used to help move the thick layers through the machine evenly.

Clean sewing machine needles and scissor blades often. Apply alcohol to a cotton ball and wipe needles and blades clean.

Clean sewing machine and work surface after each session to remove small fiber particles.

Fleece comes in a variety of weights. For blankets that are made with two layers, use lightweight fleece with no visible nap.

Laundering Fleece

Note that fleece is damaged by heat and friction. In order to prevent your blanket from becoming matted and scratchy, wash in cold water on gentle cycle and never use bleach or fabric softener in the wash cycle. Air-dry after washing. Never iron.

Basic Instructions

Choosing a Marking Tool

Choose an ink or chalk color that will contrast with your fleece. There are several marking tools from which to choose including the following:

Air-soluble marking pen—Similar to a felt-tipped pen, it makes a fine line of ink that will dissipate after one to three days. You can also remove the ink with water. This pen is easy to use, but lines must be redrawn if your project takes more than a few days to complete.

Water-soluble marking pen—Similar to a felt-tipped pen, it makes a fine line of ink that disappears with water. Ink is removed by blotting marked lines with a wet cloth or by spritzing lightly. Because fleece is polyester and has a nap, the ink lines sometimes reappear after treating, and will require a second or third water treatment.

Tailor's chalk pencil—This is a pencil with chalk "lead." Lines drawn with chalk are fainter than those drawn with ink but erase easily; simply brush lightly with a soft cloth.

Chalk wheel marker—This is a tube with a small rolling wheel in the tip. The center of the marker is filled with loose chalk that is dispersed through the moving tip. This chalk line is more prominent than one drawn with a chalk pencil and works great with a straightedge ruler. However, the embedded wheel makes it difficult to draw tight curves or notches. Remove lines by brushing with a soft cloth.

Using a Rotary Cutter

Place the fleece on a self-healing cutting mat and align the ruler with the marked line. Using the ruler as a guide, hold the ruler firmly in place with fingers clear of the edge. Draw the blade along the ruler's edge. Rotary blades are especially sharp. With the proper placement and pressure, you can cut through two layers of fleece at the same time. Take care to never leave the blade uncovered. Retract the blade when you place the cutter on the work surface.

Making Templates

Place the template material on the pattern given and use a pencil to trace along the lines of the pattern. Cut along the marked lines.

Trimming Corners

Trim square corners as shown in Figure 1 to reduce bulk.

Figure 1

Figure 2

Trim round corners as shown in Figure 2 to reduce bulk.

Mitering Corners

A mitered corner has a 45-degree angle fold or seam at the corner. It is used in this book when trims or edgings continue around a corner.

Fold the trim at the corner to form a 45-degree angle (Figure 3). This fold may be stitched and trimmed to reduce bulk (Figure 4) or the folded part may be folded under the trim and pressed to one side or the other (Figure 5). If the trim is wide enough, the fold on the top side may be hand-stitched closed (Figure 6).

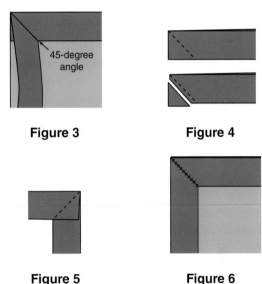

Figure 3

Figure 4

Figure 5

Figure 6

If turning the backing to the top side and mitering corners, a half-square triangle is trimmed from the backing close to but not touching the corner point of the blanket top (Figure 7). The two backing sides are then folded up and over to the top side with edges butting at the corner to form the miter (Figure 8).

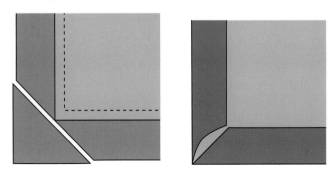

Figure 7

Figure 8

Hand-stitch the matched edges together at the corner to finish (Figure 9).

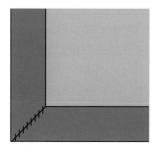

Figure 9

Stitch Instructions

Whipstitch

Whipstitches are small, even hand stitches that are used to attach trims or bindings, or to join raw edges together. Working left to right, bring needle up from wrong side at A, down at B, up at C, down at D, etc. Pull stitches snug as you stitch.

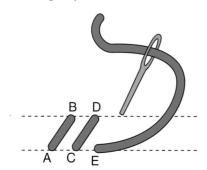

Whipstitch

Running Stitch

Running stitches are short, close hand stitches in a straight line used to hold layers together.

Running Stitch

Basting Stitch

Basting stitches are long hand stitches that are worked the same as a running stitch, but are longer and easily removed. Since layered fleece is bulky, basting layers together makes it possible to work on two layers as if they were one. Working right to left, insert the needle down at 1, up at 2 and down again at 3 making stitches at least 1" long.

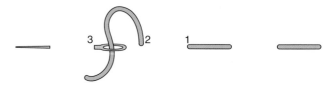

Basting Stitch

Gathering Stitch

Adjust machine to gathering stitch. On most machines this is the longest possible stitch length. Stitch one seam ½ inch from the raw edge. Stitch a parallel seam ¼ inch from the edge. Pick up both lower threads and pull fabric along the thread to gather (Figure 10).

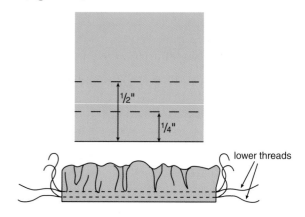

Figure 10

Tacking Stitch

A tacking stitch is used in this book for the Origami edging on page 56. A series of small and closely spaced stitches are used to secure the final loop to the blanket back.

Ladder Stitch

A ladder stitch is used to close seam allowance openings. Knot thread ends and bring thread to front from wrong side at seam allowance. Take a small stitch in one side of the opening at seam allowance. Take a second stitch from the opposite seam allowance and pull closed. Take stitches alternately from both sides of seam. Knot at end of opening.

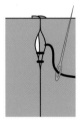

Ladder Stitch

Blanket Stitch

A blanket stitch is a useful and decorative stitch often used to hold one applied layer to a lower layer, as for appliqué. It can be done by hand or by machine. Contrasting or matching thread can be used, or you may choose a heavier thread to showcase the stitches.

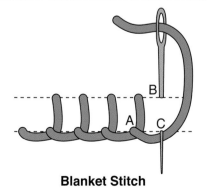

Blanket Stitch

Three-Step Zigzag Stitch

The three-step zigzag stitch makes a good seam finish, especially for stretchy materials. It has three stitches in each zig and zag.

Three-Step Zigzag Stitch

The Basic Blanket

Blankets can be made from two layers of fleece or only one. Check your edge pattern to see how many layers the edging was designed for.

Determine the size of blanket you want to create. Remember that fleece is generally 58–60 inches wide. So you can make a blanket at least the width of the fabric minus the selvage (approximately 56–58 inches) by a desired length without piecing the fleece. This width will make twin-size blankets, throws, or toddler and baby blankets.

Choose the type of edge finish desired. Read through the finished pattern for any special cutting instructions for blanket top and backing. Determine yardage for either a double- or single-layer blanket. Be sure to purchase slightly more length than you require to compensate for uneven cuts on the purchased piece.

You should treat fleece as fabric with a nap when purchasing yardage listed on patterns.

Straighten at least one cut end of the fleece. Measure the length desired from this end and trim away excess.

Now you are ready to apply the desired edge finish referring to the specific edge-finish instructions. The following instructions on page 8 are for a two-layer sample blanket made with the Loops & More edging.

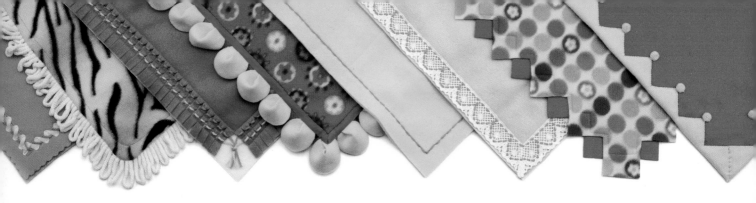

Loops & More Baby Blanket

Finished Size
36 x 36 inches

Materials
- 2¼ yards light green fleece for blanket top and backing
- Assorted ribbons and trims in various widths to coordinate with blanket top and backing
- Basic sewing supplies and equipment

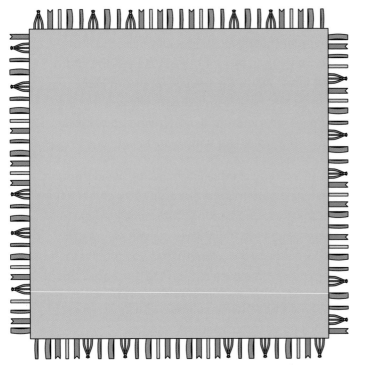

Loops & More
Placement Diagram 36" x 36"

Cutting

From light green fleece:
Cut 2 (37-inch) squares for blanket top and backing.

From assorted trims/ribbons:
Cut into 3-inch lengths for single layers and 6-inch lengths for loops.

Assembly
1. Refer to Loops & More edging on page 21 to complete the blanket. ●

Straight Path

Materials
- Fleece for blanket top and backing*
- Rotary cutter with Skip-Stitch® blade
- 2 colors acrylic yarn that contrast with fleece*
- Basic sewing supplies and equipment

Sample was made with yellow fleece for top and backing, and orange and blue acrylic yarn.

Assembly
Refer to the General Instructions as needed for construction methods and cutting fleece to size.

1. Mark a line on the blanket top 1 inch from outside edge.

2. With wrong sides together, center the blanket top on the backing. Using the rotary cutter with a Skip-Stitch® blade, cut along the marked line through both layers to make small slits for lacing (Figure 1).

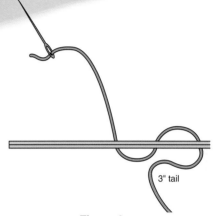

3" tail

Figure 2

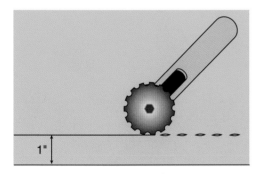

1"

Figure 1

3. Cut a 24–28-inch length of one color yarn. Thread the yarn through a tapestry needle and insert it into the backing side of the blanket. Draw it through an opening to the top side leaving a 3-inch yarn tail (Figure 2). Continue weaving the yarn through the openings with a running stitch through both layers (Figure 3).

Figure 3

4. Attach a second length of yarn to the first by knotting the yarn lengths together on the back side of the blanket. Trim yarn ends. Continue weaving and stitching around the entire blanket. Tie yarn ends together and trim ends.

5. Cut a length of the second color of yarn and insert it on the backing side, staggering the weaving and stitches (Figure 4). Repeat steps 3 and 4 with this color yarn. ●

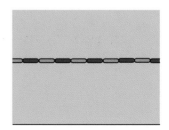

Figure 4

1-2-3 Fringe

Materials

- Fleece for blanket top and backing*
- 3 colors acrylic yarn that coordinate with fleece*
- Basic sewing supplies and equipment

Sample was made with blue plaid fleece for blanket top and backing, and purple, aqua and blue acrylic yarn for fringe.

Assembly

Refer to the General Instructions as needed for construction methods.

1. Determine desired blanket size and add 1 inch to width and length. Cut one piece of fleece each for the blanket top and backing.

2. With right sides together, center the blanket top on the backing and pin around the edges through both layers.

3. Using a ½-inch seam allowance, stitch around edge leaving an 8-inch opening along one side (Figure 1).

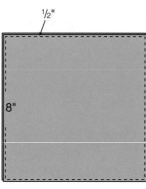

Figure 1

4. Trim the seam allowance to ¼ inch from seam line and trim corners (Figure 2).

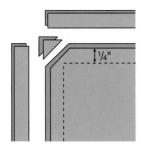

Figure 2

5. Turn right side out through the opening and straighten edges. ***Note:*** *Use a turning tool in corners if necessary.*

6. Hand-stitch the opening closed.

7. To mark tassel points, insert straight pins at regular intervals ⅜ inch from the blanket edge. Adjust spacing as necessary (Figure 3). ***Note:*** *Tassels on photo model are 1⅜ inches apart. Space them from 1¼–2 inches apart depending on the length and width of your blanket.*

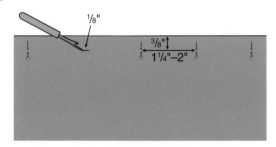

Figure 3

8. Insert a seam ripper through both layers at the first pinned site and carefully cut a slit that is large enough to accommodate the needle, approximately ⅛-inch long, again referring to Figure 3.

9. Cut one 9-inch length of each yarn color and thread all three strands through the needle. From the wrong side of the blanket, insert the needle through the slit. Draw yarn to the front of the blanket and then back down through the same hole to make a loop (Figure 4).

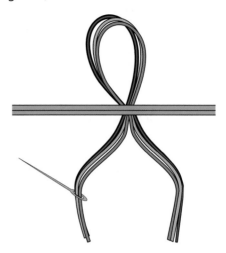

Figure 4

10. Remove the needle. Insert yarn ends through loop (Figure 5). Pull tightly and trim yarn ends even.

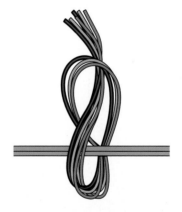

Figure 5

11. Repeat steps 8–10 at each pinned tassel point. ●

Needlepoint Lace

Materials

- Fleece for blanket top and backing*
- Open-weave 1–1½-inch-wide flat cotton lace
- Acrylic yarn*
- Basic sewing supplies and equipment

Sample was made with light green fleece for top and backing. Pink yarn was woven through 1½-inch white lace.

Assembly

Refer to the General Instructions as needed for construction methods and cutting fleece to size.

1. Draw a line on the blanket top 1½ inches from the outside edge. With wrong sides together, center the blanket top on the backing and pin along marked line through both layers.

2. Align the top edge of the lace with the marked line (Figure 1).

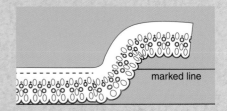

Figure 1

3. Machine-stitch along top edge of lace through all layers, folding corners to miter as you stitch. Overlap ends slightly and trim to end stitching.

4. Cut several 24–28-inch lengths of yarn. Weave one length of yarn through the lace in the desired pattern. Knot a second length of yarn to the first and trim the yarn ends, hiding knot under lace; continue weaving around the entire border. Knot yarn ends and trim. Hide knot under lace. ●

Rickrack Trick

Materials

- Fleece for blanket top*
- Contrasting fleece for blanket backing*
- Rotary cutter with scallop blade
- ¾-inch or wider rickrack*
- Acrylic yarn*
- Basic sewing supplies and equipment

*Sample was made with orange fleece for top, gray fleece for backing, yellow ¾-inch-wide rickrack and aqua acrylic yarn.

Assembly

Refer to the General Instructions as needed for construction methods and cutting fleece to size.

1. Cut around the blanket top ⅛–¼ inch from the outside edge using rotary cutter with scallop blade. Measuring from the scalloped edge, mark a line 1½ inches from the outside edge all around.

2. With wrong sides together, center the blanket top on the backing and pin along the marked line through both layers.

3. Align the top edge of the rickrack with the marked line and machine-stitch along top edge (Figure 1), folding rickrack at corners to miter. Overlap ends slightly, and trim.

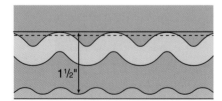

1½"

Figure 1

4. Cut one 24–28-inch length of yarn. Thread the yarn through a tapestry needle and insert it under the top edge of the rickrack. Weave the yarn under and then over the rickrack (Figure 2). Cut and knot a second length of yarn to the first and trim the yarn ends; adjust to hide the knot under the rickrack.

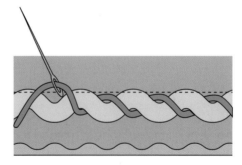

Figure 2

5. Repeat step 4 around the entire rickrack border. At end, knot and trim yarn ends, hiding knot under rickrack.

6. Machine-stitch along the bottom edge of the rickrack (Figure 3). ●

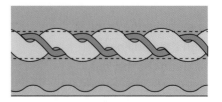

Figure 3

Border Crown

Materials

- Fleece for blanket top*
- Contrasting fleece for blanket backing*
- Contrasting-color ½-inch-wide bias tape*
- Rotary cutter with scallop blade
- Basic sewing supplies and equipment

*Sample was made with pink-with-white-dots fleece for top, light green fleece for backing and blue bias tape.

Assembly

Refer to the General Instructions as needed for construction methods and cutting fleece to size.

1. Using rotary cutter with scallop blade, cut around the blanket top ½–¾ inch from the outside edge. Mark a line 1¼ inches from the trimmed edge.

2. With wrong sides together, center the blanket top on the backing and pin along the marked line through both layers.

3. Open one folded edge of the bias tape. Align the fold line of the bias tape along the marked line and, starting 1 inch from the end, machine-stitch along fold line (Figure 1).

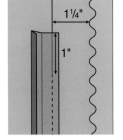

Figure 1

4. Fold bias tape at corners to make mitered corners and continue stitching.

5. Overlap ends of bias tape slightly, turning under the bottom overlapped edge to eliminate the raw end (Figure 2).

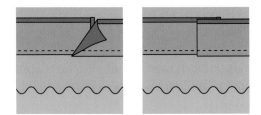

Figure 2

6. Refold the bias tape at the stitched line and fold opposite edge under. Using a small zigzag stitch, machine-stitch along the opposite edge (Figure 3). ●

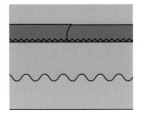

Figure 3

Cockleshells

Materials

- Fleece for blanket top*
- Contrasting fleece for blanket backing*
- Chenille yarn*
- Basic sewing supplies and equipment

Sample was made with light blue fleece for top, aqua fleece for backing and white/pastels chenille yarn.

Project Note: *Finished size of blanket will determine the required yardage of chenille yarn needed. Measure the entire length of the marked line in step 1 and add 2".*

Assembly

Refer to the General Instructions as needed for preparing templates, cutting fleece top and backing and other construction methods.

1. Mark a line 1¼ inches from the outside edge of the blanket top.

2. Prepare template for the scallops shape using pattern on page 60.

3. Center the scallops template at the center of one edge of the blanket top (Figure 1).

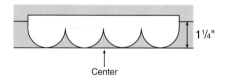

1¼"

Center

Figure 1

4. Working from the center to the corners, mark around the edge of the template until a complete arc will not fit. Mark the remaining three sides. Square the corners referring to Figure 2.

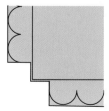

Figure 2

5. Cut along the marked scallops line.

6. With wrong sides together, center the blanket top on the backing and pin along the marked line through both layers.

7. Place the yarn on the marked line and, with a three-step zigzag stitch, machine-stitch along the yarn. Overlap ends slightly and trim. ●

Jersey Chain

Materials

- Fleece for blanket top*
- Contrasting fleece for blanket backing*
- Print jersey to coordinate with blanket-top fleece
- Water-soluble stabilizer*
- Basic sewing supplies and equipment

*Sample was made with orange fleece for top, ivory fleece for backing and Solvy™ water-soluble stabilizer from Sulky®.

Assembly

Refer to the General Instructions as needed for preparing template, cutting fleece to size and other construction methods.

1. With wrong sides together, center the blanket top on the backing.

2. Cut 3½-inch-wide strips of stabilizer. With a water-soluble marking pen, trace the lines of the stitching pattern on page 62 onto the stabilizer. Adjust design as needed to meet at the center of blanket sides.

3. Cut 3½-inch-wide strips of jersey. Place the strips along the edges of the blanket top, overlapping ends slightly at breaks (Figure 1).

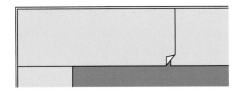

Figure 1

4. Place the marked stabilizer strips on top of the jersey strips and pin through all layers. Machine-stitch along the marked lines (Figure 2).

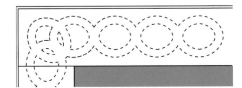

Figure 2

5. Cut away large sections of stabilizer, then immerse the blanket sides in water to remove the remaining stabilizer. Let dry.

6. Carefully cut through jersey layer only, to within ⅛ inch of stitching lines (Figure 3).

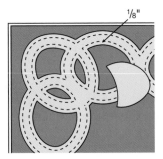 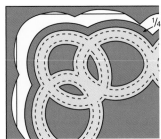

Figure 3   **Figure 4**

7. Carefully cut away outer edge of the blanket top only, to within ¼ inch of stitching lines (Figure 4). ●

Twist & Shout

Materials

- Fleece for blanket top*
- Contrasting fleece for blanket backing*
- Basic sewing supplies and equipment

Sample was made with yellow fleece for top and turquoise fleece for backing.

Assembly

Refer to the General Instructions as needed for construction methods.

1. Determine desired blanket size and add 1 inch to width and 1 inch to length. Cut one piece of fleece each for blanket top and backing.

2. Mark a line 2½ inches from edges of the blanket top.

3. With wrong sides together, center the blanket top on the backing and pin along the marked line through both layers. Machine-stitch on the marked line.

4. Starting 2½ inches in from the corners, cut 1-inch-wide perpendicular slits in the blanket top only, to within ⅛ inch of the stitched seam (Figure 1). Cut out squares at seam corners. (Figure 2)

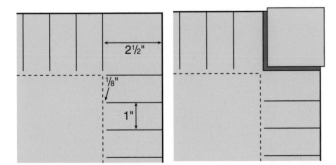

Figure 1   **Figure 2**

5. Starting at the end of one side, twist one strip and machine-stitch in place approximately 1 inch from the inner seam line (Figure 3). Using a continuous seam, turn and stitch remaining strips to complete one side. Repeat with the remaining three sides.

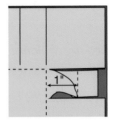

Figure 3

6. Trim the backing fleece to within ½ inch of strip ends along sides and at corners. ●

Wrapped Steps

Materials

- Dark fleece for blanket top*
- Contrasting fleece for blanket backing*
- Contrasting pompoms*
- Basic sewing supplies and equipment

Sample was made with dark pink fleece for top, light green fleece for backing and pink pompoms.

Project Notes: *Finished size of blanket will determine the required number of pompoms needed.*

Because the wrapped corners of the blanket need to be mirror images, make square blankets only.

Warning: *Pompoms are not recommended for baby blankets because of potential choking hazard.*

Assembly

Refer to the General Instructions as needed for preparing template and other construction methods.

1. Determine desired blanket size and cut one square of dark fleece for blanket top. Cut one square of contrasting fleece that is 3¾ inches larger than blanket top for backing.

2. Prepare the points template using pattern on page 60.

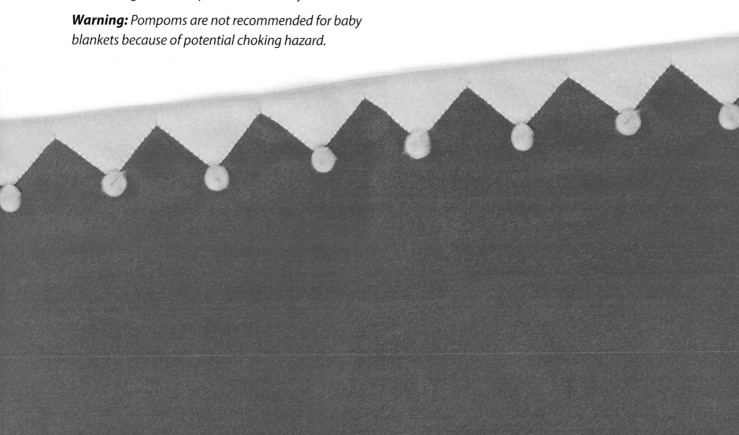

3. Center the template on one edge of the backing and mark around the pointed edge of the template (Figure 1). Continue to mark the edge from the center out to each corner. Repeat on the remaining three sides.

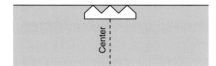

Figure 1

4. Cut along the marked lines.

5. With wrong sides together, center the blanket top on the backing and pin along the edge through both layers. Machine-stitch ½ inch from outside edge of blanket top (Figure 2).

Figure 2

6. Trim corners from the backing at a 45-degree angle (Figure 3).

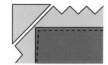

Figure 3

7. Fold backing points over the edge of the blanket top and pin through all layers (Figure 4). Butt straight edges at corners.

Figure 4

8. Use thread to match the backing to hand-stitch the edges of the points to the blanket top and at the corners (Figure 5).

Figure 5

9. To finish, tack a pompom in place at the tip of each point. ●

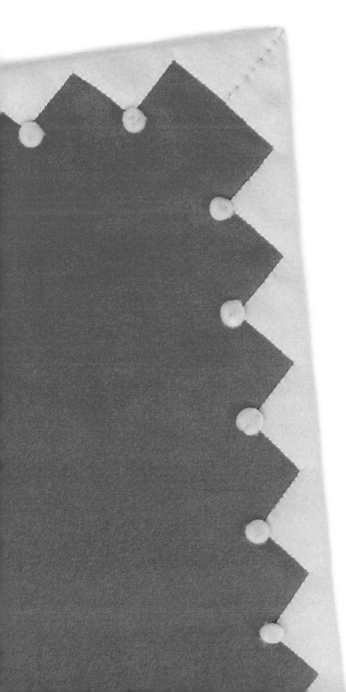

Baby Bump

Materials

- Fleece for blanket top*
- Contrasting fleece for blanket backing*
- Cotton cord
- Zipper foot
- Basic sewing supplies and equipment

Sample was made with gray fleece for top, dark blue fleece for backing and ⅜" cotton cord.

Project Note: *Finished size of blanket will determine the required yardage of cord needed. Measure the length of the entire outside edge and add 2".*

Assembly

Refer to the General Instructions as needed for construction methods.

1. Determine desired blanket size and add 3 inches to the length and width. Cut one piece of fleece each for the blanket top and backing.

2. Starting in the center of one side, place the cord end on the wrong-side edge of blanket top and wrap with fleece edge to cover cord; pin through both layers of fleece (Figure 1). Continue pinning to corner.

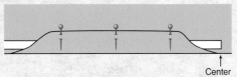

Figure 1

3. Using a zipper foot, machine-stitch along cut edge of fleece, close to cord, stopping 2 inches from the corner (Figure 2).

Figure 2

4. Bend the cord around the corner. Wrap and pin along the adjoining side; continue stitching, stopping ½ inch from the first corner. Move to the adjoining side and continue stitching, starting ½ inch from the corner (Figure 3). **Note:** *It is difficult to stitch around the corner with the zipper foot, so stitch as close to the corner as you can to hold layers together.*

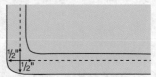

Figure 3

5. Repeat steps 3 and 4 on all sides.

6. To end, trim cord ends to meet and continue stitching to starting point (Figure 4).

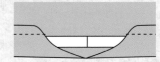

Figure 4

7. Trim seam allowance to within ¼ inch of seam.

8. With wrong sides together, center the blanket top on the backing and pin inside the seam line through all layers.

9. Starting and stopping ½ inch from corners, machine-stitch layers together along the wrapped seam (Figure 5).

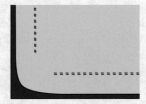

Figure 5

10. Trim backing as desired, leaving a margin of the backing all around as a contrasting edge. ●

Loops & More

Materials

- Fleece for blanket top*
- Fleece, flannel or lightweight cotton jersey for blanket backing*
- Assorted grosgrain ribbons in various widths to coordinate with blanket top*
- Assorted satin ribbons in various widths to coordinate with blanket top*
- ⅜-inch-wide or wider rickrack to coordinate with blanket top*
- Basic sewing supplies and equipment

*Sample was made with light green fleece for blanket top, white lightweight cotton jersey for blanket backing, ¼-inch-wide and ⅝-inch-wide grosgrain ribbons, ⅜-inch-wide and ⅝-inch-wide satin ribbons, and ⅜-inch-wide rickrack.

Project Note: *Preshrink lightweight cotton jersey if using for backing fabric.*

Refer to Loops & More Baby Blanket *on page 8 for instructions for a 36" square blanket.*

Assembly

Refer to the General Instructions as needed for construction methods.

1. Determine desired blanket size and add 1 inch to width and length. Cut one piece of fleece for blanket top and one piece of backing fabric.

2. For single-layer ribbon and rickrack fringe, cut 2½-inch lengths. For ribbon loops, cut 5-inch lengths and fold in half.

3. Pin fringe and loops along edges of blanket top, spacing as desired, overlapping ribbons at corners; baste in place ½ inch from the edge of the blanket top (Figure 1).

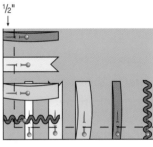

Figure 1

4. Aligning edges and with right sides facing, place blanket top and backing together and pin around edges through all layers. Make sure to keep ends of fringe and loops away from seam line.

5. Using a ½-inch seam allowance, machine-stitch through all layers leaving an 8-inch opening along one side. Trim corners (Figure 2).

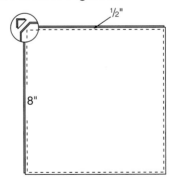

Figure 2

6. Turn right side out through the opening and straighten sides and corners. **Note:** *Use a turning tool in corners if necessary.*

7. Hand-stitch opening closed. ●

Bunny Hop

Materials

- Fleece for a 1-layer blanket*
- Chenille ball-fringe trim*
- Yarn for tying corners*
- Basic sewing supplies and equipment

Sample was made with light green fleece, white ball-fringe trim and lavender yarn.

Project Note: *The finished size of blanket will determine required yardage for chenille ball-fringe trim. Add 2 inches to the length of the four sides of blanket.*

Assembly

Refer to the General Instructions as needed for construction methods.

1. Determine desired blanket size and add 3 inches to width and length. Cut one piece of fleece.

2. Place the ball-fringe trim on the work surface and measure to determine the spacing between chenille balls for perpendicular slits (Figure 1). *Note: The trim used in the sample has chenille balls that are spaced 1¹⁄₁₆ inches apart.*

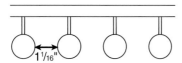

Figure 1

3. On the wrong side of fleece, draw a line 1½ inches from outside edge all around.

4. Cut perpendicular slits from the outside edge to the marked line, spaced using distance determined in step 2; cut squares from corners of fleece (Figure 2).

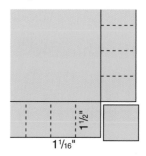

Figure 2

5. Starting in the center of one side, place the bottom of the header of the ball-fringe trim on the marked line and slide a chenille ball through each slit (Figure 3).

Figure 3

6. Fold up the tabs along the header of the trim as shown in Figure 4. Pin through all layers.

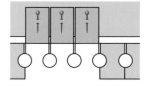

Figure 4

7. Overlap at corners referring to Figure 5.

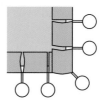

Figure 5

8. With one continuous seam and a medium zigzag stitch, machine-stitch through all layers close to the edges of the folded tabs (Figure 6).

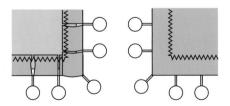

Figure 6

9. Tie a yarn bow around each corner chenille ball to secure (Figure 7). ●

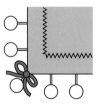

Figure 7

Picket Fence

Materials

- Print fleece for blanket top*
- Contrasting fleece for blanket backing*
- Basic sewing supplies and equipment

Sample was made with yellow print fleece for top and dark pink fleece for backing.

Assembly

Refer to the General Instructions as needed for preparing templates, cutting fleece pieces and other construction methods.

1. Prepare templates for A and B corners, edge and stitching using patterns on pages 58 and 59.

2. Place the A corner template on one corner of the blanket top and mark around the edge of the template (Figure 1). Repeat on an adjacent corner.

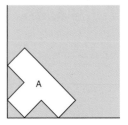

Figure 1

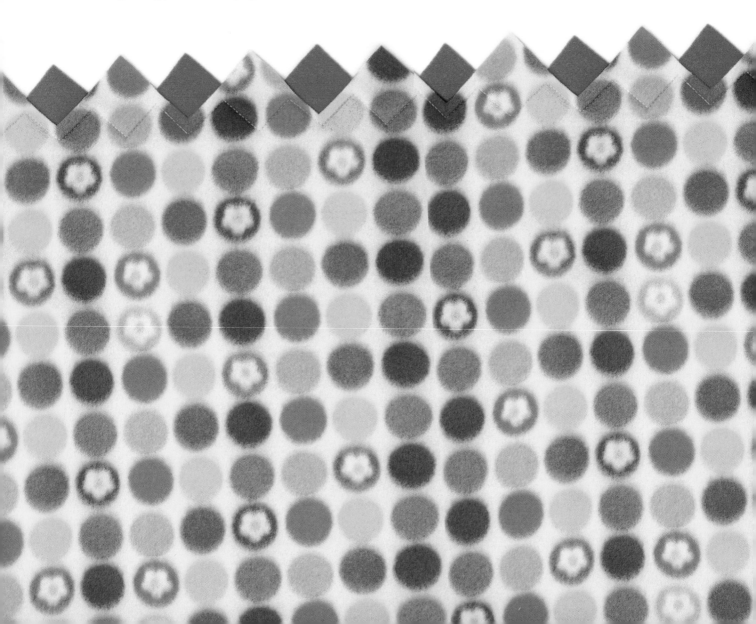

3. Working toward the center of the side edge between the two marked corners, use the edge template to mark the design until a complete point will not fit. Join the points at the center (Figure 2).

Figure 2

4. Repeat steps 2 and 3 with the remaining corners and sides.

5. Cut along the marked lines on all sides.

6. Repeat step 2 with the B corner template on the blanket backing to mark two adjacent corners (Figure 3).

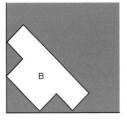

Figure 3

7. Repeat step 2 with the edge template, joining the points at the center (Figure 4).

Figure 4

8. Repeat steps 6 and 7 with the remaining corners and sides.

9. Cut along marked lines on all sides.

10. Mark the stitching line on the blanket top using the stitching template (Figure 5).

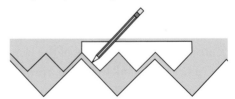

Figure 5

11. With wrong sides together, center the blanket top on the backing and pin along marked line through both layers.

12. Machine-stitch layers together along the marked line. ●

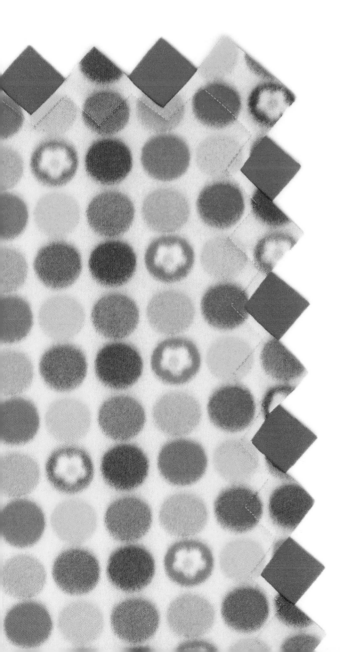

Wrapped Pie Crust

Materials
- Print fleece for blanket top*
- Contrasting fleece for blanket backing*
- Contrasting-color embroidery floss*
- Basic sewing supplies and equipment

Sample was made with orange print fleece for top, cream solid fleece for backing and blue embroidery floss.

Project Note: *Because the wrapped corners of the blanket need to be mirror images, make square blankets only.*

Assembly
Refer to the General Instructions as needed for making templates and other construction methods.

1. Determine desired blanket size and cut one square of print fleece for blanket top. Cut one square of contrasting fleece for backing 3¾ inches larger than the blanket top.

2. Prepare the wave template using pattern on page 60.

3. Center the template on one edge of the backing and mark around the curved edge of the template (Figure 1). Continue to mark the edge from the center out to each corner. Repeat on the remaining three sides.

Center

Figure 1

4. Cut along the marked line (Figure 2).

Figure 2

5. With wrong sides together, center the blanket top on the backing and pin along the edge through both layers. Machine-stitch ½ inch from outside edge of the top layer (Figure 3).

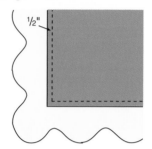

½"

Figure 3

6. Trim corners from the backing at a 45-degree angle (Figure 4).

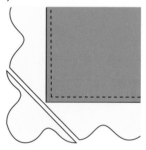

Figure 4

7. Fold backing curves over blanket top edges and pin through all layers (Figure 5). Butt the straight edges at the corners.

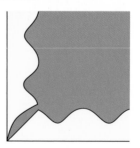

Figure 5

8. Using 2 strands of embroidery floss, stitch the folded-over backing edges to the blanket top using a blanket stitch (Figure 6).

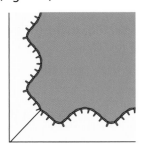

Figure 6

9. Hand-stitch corners closed with thread to match backing fleece (Figure 7). ●

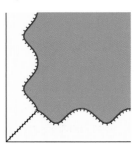

Figure 7

Nook & Cranny

Materials

- Fleece for blanket top and backing*
- Fleece for edging*
- Basic sewing supplies and equipment

Sample was made with gray fleece for blanket top and backing, and dark pink fleece for edging.

Assembly

Refer to the General Instructions as needed for construction methods.

1. Determine desired blanket size and add 1 inch to the width and length. Cut one piece of fleece each for the blanket top and backing.

2. With right sides together, center the blanket top on the backing and pin around edges through both layers. Using a ½-inch seam allowance, machine-stitch through all layers leaving an 8-inch opening along one side (Figure 1). Trim corners.

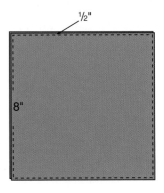

Figure 1

6. Unpin strip and insert the edge of blanket inside the folded edging strip, placing so that corners of blanket poke through the triangles on strip; miter strip at corners on front and back as needed to lie flat (Figure 4). Overlap strip ends ½ inch at beginning and end. Pin through all layers.

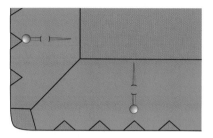

Figure 4

3. Turn right side out through the opening and straighten sides and corners. **Note:** *Use a turning tool in corners if necessary.* Hand-stitch opening closed.

4. To determine the length of the edging strip, measure around the outside edge of the blanket and add 1 inch. Cut 4-inch-wide strips from fleece for edging. Overlap and stitch strips on the short ends to make one long strip (Figure 2). **Note:** *Cut strips across 54-inch width of fabric to keep piecing to a minimum.*

Figure 2

7. Machine-stitch edging through all layers ¾ inch from blanket edge (Figure 5).

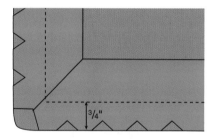

Figure 5

5. Fold edging strip in half along length and pin raw edges together for stability while cutting. Cut triangle-shaped notches in the folded edge of the strip as shown in Figure 3.

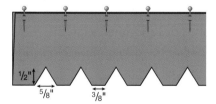

Figure 3

8. Evenly trim the edging to within ¼ inch of the seam on the blanket front and blanket back (Figure 6). ●

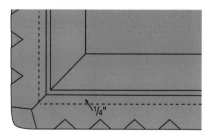

Figure 6

Chenille Skirt

Materials

- Print fleece for blanket top*
- Fleece, flannel or lightweight cotton jersey for blanket backing*
- Chenille yarn*
- Basic sewing supplies and equipment

Sample was made with tiger print fleece for blanket top, white cotton jersey for backing and yellow chenille yarn for fringe.

Project Note: *Preshrink cotton flannel fabric if using for backing fabric.*

Assembly

Refer to the General Instructions as needed for preparing template and other construction methods.

1. Determine desired blanket size and add 1 inch. Cut one piece of print fleece for blanket top and one piece of backing fabric.

2. Prepare the corner trimming template using pattern on page 58.

3. Place the template on each corner of both the blanket top and backing, and mark around edge. Cut along marked lines to make round corners (Figure 1).

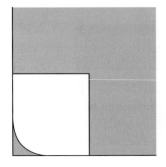

Figure 1

4. Working in 4-inch sections, make 2-inch long yarn loops along edge of the blanket top. Distribute evenly and baste yarn in place ½ inch from edges. (Figure 2)

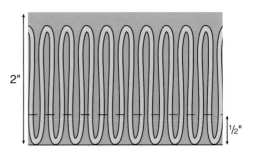

2"

½"

Figure 2

5. Overlap inside ends of loops at corners and baste in place (Figure 3). Continue around entire edge of blanket top.

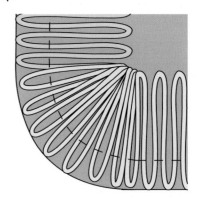

Figure 3

6. With right sides together, align the edges of the blanket top with the edges of backing; pin along the edges through all layers.

7. Using a ½-inch seam allowance, machine-stitch layers together leaving an 8-inch opening along one side (Figure 4). Trim corners. Remove basting stitches.

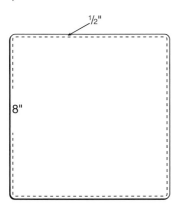

Figure 4

8. Turn right side out through the opening and straighten sides and corners. Whipstitch the opening closed.

9. Pin along seam through both layers. Machine-topstitch through all layers ⅝ inch from outside edge (Figure 5). ●

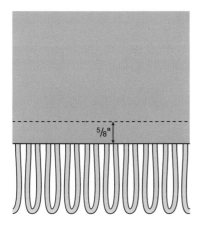

Figure 5

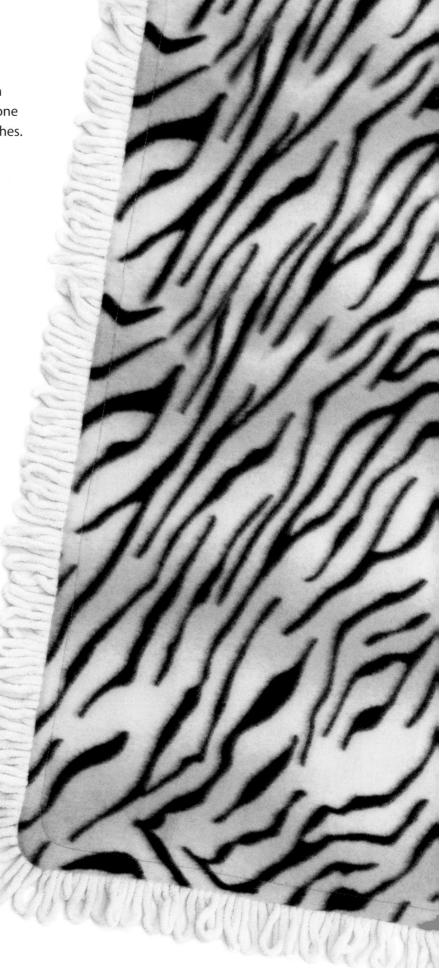

Gather Round

Materials

- Fleece for blanket top*
- Fleece, flannel or lightweight cotton jersey for blanket backing*
- Chiffon for ruffle*
- Basic sewing supplies and equipment

Sample was made with light green-with-dots fleece for blanket top, white lightweight cotton jersey for blanket backing and melon-with-white dots chiffon for ruffle.

Project Note: *Preshrink cotton flannel fabric if using for backing fabric.*

Assembly With No Breaks at Corners

Refer to the General Instructions as needed for construction methods.

1. Determine desired blanket size and add 1 inch to width and length. Cut one piece of fleece for blanket top and one piece of backing fabric.

2. Cut 4-inch-wide bias strips from chiffon for ruffle (Figure 1).

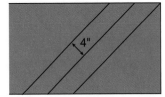

4"

Figure 1

3. Join the strips to make one long strip (Figure 2); press seams open. **Note:** *To determine the required length, measure all four sides of the blanket and multiply by 1.5. For example, a 36-inch-square blanket will require a 216-inch bias strip.*

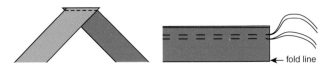

← fold line

Figure 2   **Figure 3**

4. Fold the bias strip in half along length with wrong sides together; press and pin long edges together. Machine-stitch two rows of gathering stitches along pinned edge, leaving long thread tails (Figure 3).

5. Pull two bottom threads to gather the ruffle to fit the sides. **Note:** *For example, a 36-inch square blanket will require a 144-inch gathered strip.* Distribute the gathers evenly.

6. Pin the gathered strip to the blanket top, referring to Figure 4 to turn corners.

Figure 4

7. Machine-baste the gathered strip in place ½ inch from the edges, starting and stopping stitching 6 inches from the beginning and end of the strip (Figure 5).

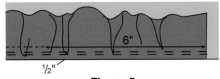

6"

½"

Figure 5

8. Join the ends of the strip with right sides together, gather to fit the remaining edge and baste in place (Figure 6).

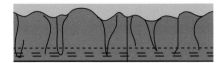

Figure 6

9. With right sides together, align the edges of the blanket top with the backing. Pin along edges through all layers. Using a ½-inch seam allowance, machine-stitch through all layers leaving an 8-inch opening along one side as shown in Figure 7; trim corners. Remove basting stitches.

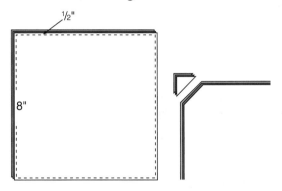

Figure 7

10. Turn right side out through the opening and straighten sides and corners. ***Note:*** *Use a turning tool in corners if necessary.* Hand-stitch opening closed.

Assembly With Breaks at Corners

Refer to the General Instructions as needed for construction methods.

1. Refer to steps 1 and 2 of Assembly With No Breaks at Corners to create blanket top and backing, and to cut bias strips for ruffle.

2. Determine the length of each side of the blanket and multiply each of those measurements by 1.5 to determine the length of bias needed for each ruffle. Join the bias strips to create ruffle strips in the required lengths.

3. Fold one ruffle strip in half along length with right sides together; pin short ends together. Stitch a

straight ½-inch seam at each end of the strip to make square finished ends. Trim excess fabric from end and bottom corner (Figure 8). Turn strip right side out; press and pin long edges together.

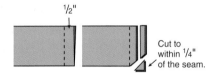

Figure 8

4. Repeat step 3 with the remaining ruffle strips.

5. Machine-stitch two rows of gathering stitches along raw edges of each strip, leaving long thread tails. Gather each strip as in step 5 of Assembly With No Breaks at Corners.

6. Pin a gathered strip to each side of the blanket top, overlapping at corners (Figure 9). Machine-baste in place ½ inch from edges, moving the overlapped ends to avoid catching in the seam.

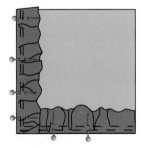

Figure 9

7. Finish the blanket referring to steps 9 and 10 of Assembly With No Breaks at Corners. ●

Ruched Road

Materials

- Print fleece for blanket top and backing*
- Lightweight cotton jersey for ruffle*
- Basic sewing supplies and equipment

*Sample was made with red print fleece for blanket top and backing, and white cotton jersey for ruffle.

Assembly With No Breaks at Corners

Refer to the General Instructions as needed for construction methods and cutting fleece to size.

1. With wrong sides together, center the blanket top on the backing and pin around edges through both layers. Baste layers together ¼ inch from edge through both layers.

2. Cut 2½-inch bias strips from jersey for ruffle (Figure 1).

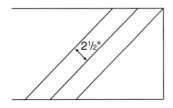

Figure 1

3. Join the strips to make one long strip (Figure 2); press seams open. **Note:** *To determine the required strip length, measure all four sides of the blanket and multiply the total by 1.5. For example, a 36-inch square blanket will require a 216-inch bias strip.*

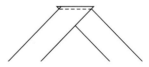

Figure 2

4. Mark a line along the length of the center of the strip. Machine-stitch along the marked line using a gathering stitch and leaving long thread tails (Figure 3).

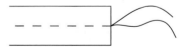

Figure 3

5. Pull the bottom thread to gather the ruffle to size. **Note:** *For example, a 36-inch-square blanket will require a 144-inch gathered strip.* Distribute the gathers evenly.

6. Pin the gathered strip to the blanket through both layers with ¾ inch of strip extending beyond blanket edges (Figure 4) and folding at corners to turn (Figure 5). Overlap the ends of the gathered strip slightly.

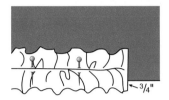

Figure 4

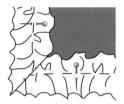

Figure 5

7. Using a three-step zigzag stitch, machine-stitch along the gathered seam.

Assembly With Breaks at Corners
Refer to the General Instructions as needed for construction methods.

1. Refer to step 1 of Assembly With No Breaks at Corners to cut fleece.

2. Cut 2½-inch bias strips for ruffle as in Figure 1. Join strips to make strips to fit each side of the blanket. *Note: To determine the required length, measure one side of the blanket and multiply by 1.5. For example, a 36-inch square blanket will require four 54-inch bias strips.* Press seams open.

3. Mark a line along the length of the center of each strip. Machine-stitch along the marked line on each strip using a gathering stitch and leaving long thread tails.

4. Pull the bottom thread of one strip to gather to size. For example a 36-inch square will require a 35-inch gathered strip. Distribute the gathers evenly. Repeat with the remaining strips.

5. Pin one gathered strip to the blanket top with ¾ inch of long edge of gathered strip extending beyond the blanket edges and with short ends ½ inch from each corner (Figure 6). With a three-step zigzag stitch, machine-stitch along the gathered seam.

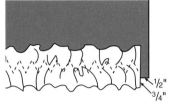

Figure 6

6. Repeat for remaining three sides. ●

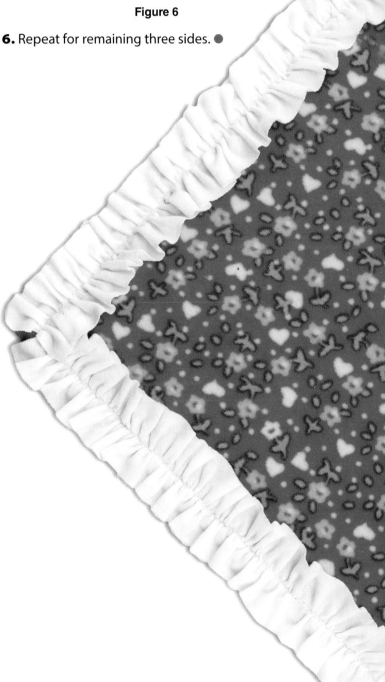

Buttercream Trim

Materials

- Fleece for blanket top*
- Flannel or lightweight cotton jersey for blanket backing*
- Fleece for icing*
- Basic sewing supplies and equipment

Sample was made with pink fleece for top, white flannel for backing and white fleece for icing.

Project Note: *Preshrink flannel if using for backing fabric.*

Assembly

Refer to the General Instructions as needed for construction methods.

1. Determine desired blanket size and add 1 inch to length and width. Cut one piece of fleece for the blanket top and one piece of backing fabric.

2. With right sides together, center the blanket top on the backing and pin around edges through both layers.

3. Using a ½-inch seam allowance, machine-stitch layers together leaving an 8-inch opening along one side (Figure 1). Trim corners.

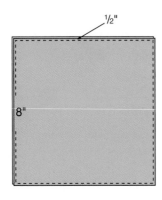

Figure 1

4. Turn right side out through the opening; straighten sides and corners. **Note:** *Use a turning tool in corners if necessary.* Hand-stitch the opening closed.

5. Mark a line on the blanket top ⅝ inch from the outside edge.

6. Cut two ⅝ x 3-inch strips from fleece. Layer the strips and stitch down the center. Repeat to make enough stitched icing strips to cover the marked line on the blanket top.

7. Open side flaps on each icing strip to cover stitches; finger press flat (Figure 2).

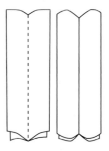

Figure 2

8. Starting in the center of one side of the blanket, align the center of one icing strip on the marked line on the blanket top (Figure 3).

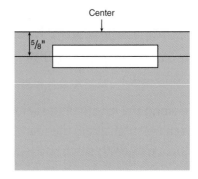

Figure 3

9. Beginning at one end of icing strip, stitch 1¼ inches through all layers (Figure 4). Backstitch each end of seam to secure. Twist the strip with the opposite side up and stitch from the opposite end for 1¼ inches through all layers (Figure 5).

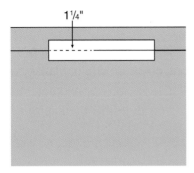

Figure 4

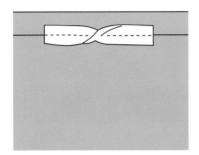

Figure 5

10. Repeat steps 7–9 to complete the icing edging on the blanket, distributing the icing strips evenly on all sides with end pieces meeting at corners (Figure 6). ●

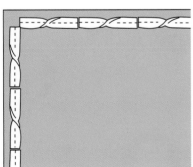

Figure 6

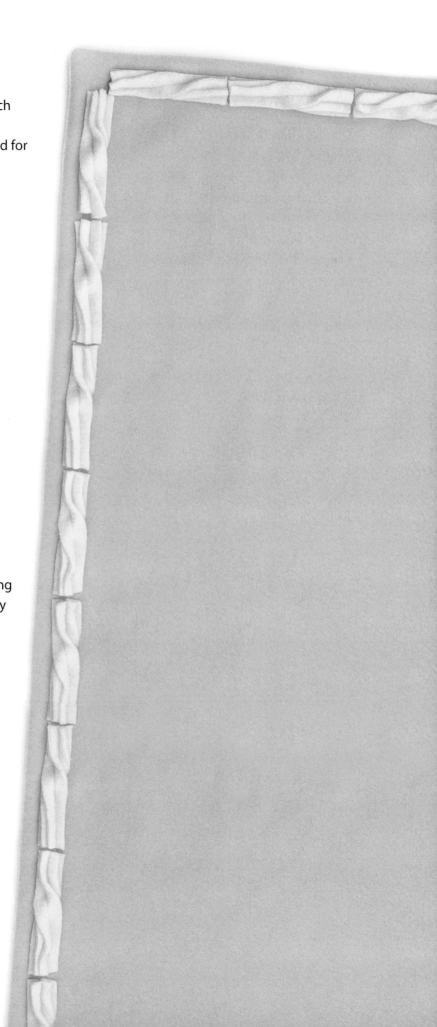

Fortune Cookies

Materials

- Print fleece for 1-layer blanket*
- Fleece for cookie edging*
- Thread to match bias tape
- ½"-wide bias tape*
- Basic sewing supplies and equipment

Sample was made with dark pink print fleece for blanket, lime green fleece for cookie edging and turquoise bias tape.

Project Note: *Finished size of blanket will determine required yardage for bias tape. Total the four sides and add 2 inches.*

Assembly

Refer to the General Instructions as needed for preparing the template, cutting fleece pieces and other construction methods.

1. Measure one outside edge of blanket and divide by 2. This will give you an approximate number of shapes needed for that side. Repeat for each side.

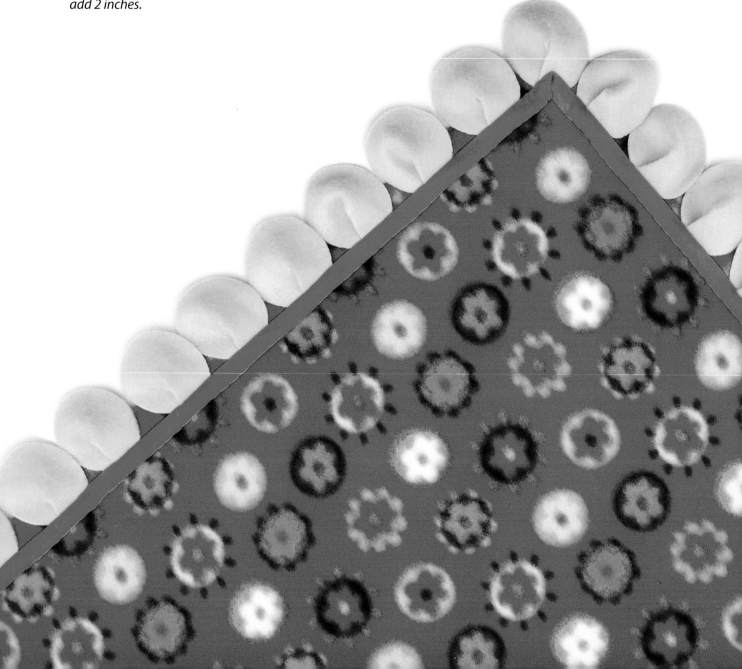

2. Prepare cookie template using pattern given on page 63. Place the template on the cookie edging fleece and mark around the outside edge. Cut along the marked line. Repeat to cut the remaining required number of cookie shapes.

3. Overlap the cookie-shape corners and pin to hold (Figure 1).

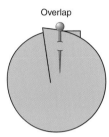

Figure 1

4. Mark a line 1 inch from the edge on the right side of the blanket all around.

5. Starting in the center and working toward the corners, place cookie shapes along the marked line, with curved edges touching. Pin to the blanket (Figure 2). Rotate shapes at corners (Figure 3).

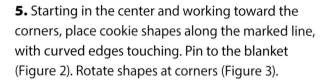

Figure 2

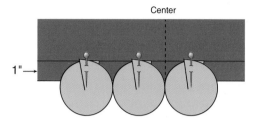

Figure 3

6. Machine-stitch through all layers ½ inch from cookie tops. Trim the cookie tops to within ¼ inch of seam (Figure 4).

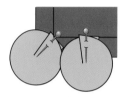

Figure 4

7. Referring to Figure 5, open the top fold of the bias tape and align the fold line slightly below the seam that holds the cookie shapes in place. Starting 1 inch from the end, machine-stitch along the fold through all layers, folding at corners to miter corners and overlapping beginning and end.

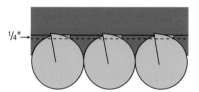

Figure 5

8. Refold bias tape to cover seam and fold opposite edge under. Hand-stitch opposite edge to the blanket. ●

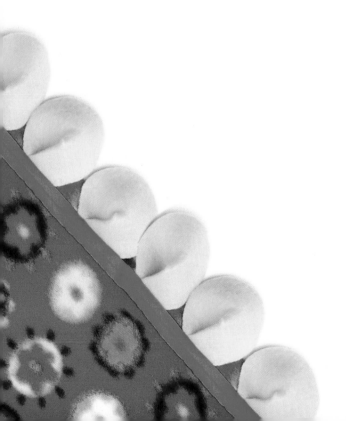

Bow Ties

Materials

- Fleece for blanket top and backing*
- ¼ yard contrasting fleece for bows*
- Acrylic yarn to match bow fleece*
- Basic sewing supplies and equipment

Sample was made with blue-with-white-dots fleece for top and backing, red fleece for bows and red yarn.

Assembly

Refer to the General Instructions as needed for construction methods and cutting fleece to size.

1. With wrong sides together, center the blanket top on the backing and pin around edges through both layers. Machine-stitch ½ inch from outside edge.

2. To determine the number of bow ties that you will need, measure the outside edge of your blanket and divide by 5. This will give you an approximate number of bow ties needed. Bow ties can be adjusted for even spacing before stitching in place.

3. Cut 2¼ x 3¾-inch rectangles from contrasting fleece using number determined in step 2.

4. Twist rectangles to make bow ties and pin to hold (Figure 1).

Figure 1

5. Starting in the center of one edge and working toward the corners, pin the bows ¼ inch from the seam (Figure 2). Adjust spacing as necessary.

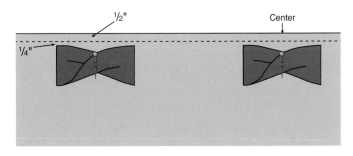

Figure 2

6. Repeat step 5 on the remaining three sides.

7. Shape bow tie ends to curve slightly and pin to secure. Machine-stitch along the curved ends through all layers (Figure 3).

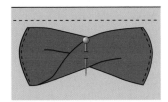

Figure 3

8. Cut one 10-inch length of yarn and tie to make a looped bow around the center of the bow tie (Figure 4). Make a secure double knot in looped bow. Trim yarn ends.

Figure 4

9. Repeat step 8 with remaining bow ties and yarn. ●

Yo-Yo Flowers

Materials

- Fleece for blanket top*
- Contrasting fleece for blanket backing*
- Green fleece for leaves
- Cotton print scraps for flowers
- Basic sewing supplies and equipment

Sample was made with white fleece for top and gray fleece for backing.

Assembly

Refer to the General Instructions as needed for preparing template, cutting fleece to size and other construction methods.

1. Trim ½ inch from the top edge and one side edge of the blanket top.

2. With wrong sides together, center the blanket top on the backing and pin around edges through both layers. Hand-stitch ¼ inch from the edge using a running stitch.

3. To determine the number of flowers needed, measure the outside edges of the blanket and divide by 3.5. This will give you an approximate number of flowers needed. Flowers can be adjusted for even spacing before stitching in place.

4. Prepare the leaf T template using pattern on page 63.

5. On green fleece, mark the desired number of T shapes determined in step 3, marking around the outside edge of the template; cut along marked lines.

6. Cut one 4-inch circle from a cotton print scrap. Referring to Figure 1, turn the outer edge to the wrong side ⅛–¼ inch. Hand-baste through both layers around the outside edge of the circle. Pull the thread tightly to cinch the stitched edge. Adjust the gathers and knot the thread end to secure. Repeat to make the number of yo-yos needed as determined in step 3.

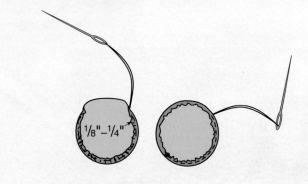

Figure 1

7. Starting in the center of one edge and working toward the corners, pin the T shapes ¾ inch from the seam. Adjust spacing as necessary. Hand-stitch in place through the centers through all layers (Figure 2).

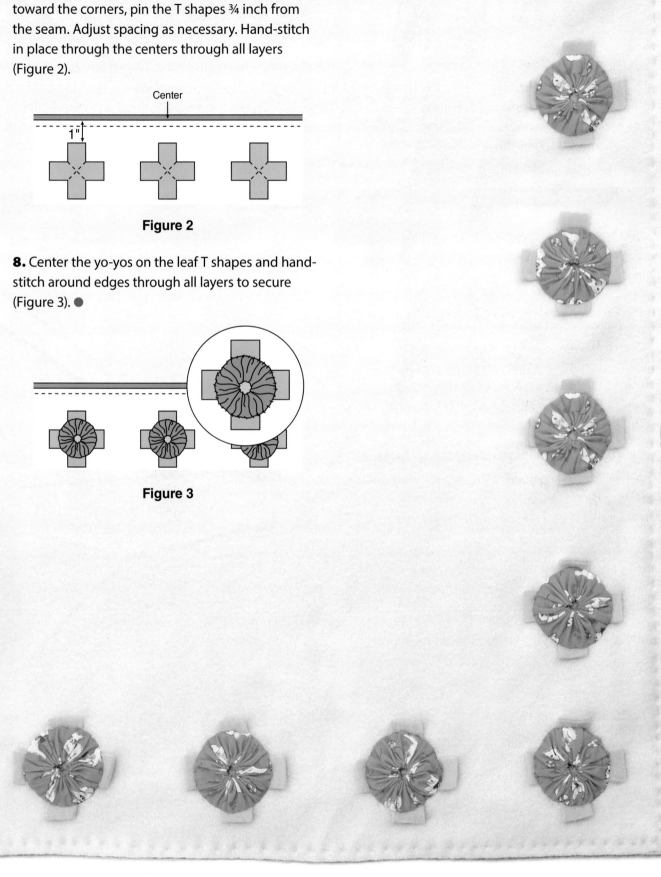

Figure 2

8. Center the yo-yos on the leaf T shapes and hand-stitch around edges through all layers to secure (Figure 3). ●

Figure 3

Cathedral Windows

Materials
- Fleece for blanket top*
- Contrasting fleece for blanket backing*
- Light-color fleece for cathedral window motifs*
- Dark-color flannel for cathedral window circles*
- Basic sewing supplies and equipment

Sample was made with pink fleece for top and white fleece for backing. Appliquéd motifs were made with white fleece and dark pink flannel.

Project Notes: *Yardage for cathedral-window motifs and circles is determined by the size of the blanket and number of motifs needed. After laundering, finger-press the flannel while still damp.*

Assembly
Refer to the General Instructions as needed for construction methods and cutting fleece to size.

1. Trim ½ inch from the top edge and one side edge of the blanket top.

2. With wrong sides together, center the blanket top on the backing and pin around the edges through both layers.

3. To determine the number of window motifs needed, measure the outside edges of the blanket and divide by 3.5. This will give you an approximate number of motifs needed. Motifs can be adjusted for even spacing before stitching in place.

4. According to number determined in step 3, cut 2¾-inch circles from the dark-colored flannel and cut 3-inch circles from light-color fleece.

5. Cut slits in fleece circles (Figure 1).

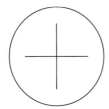

Figure 1

6. Starting in the center of one edge and working toward the corners, pin the flannel circles ½ inch from the outside edge (Figure 2). Adjust spacing as necessary.

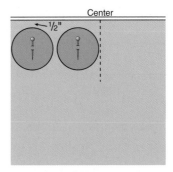

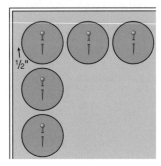

Figure 2

7. Mark stitching lines through the pinned flannel circles on the edges and corners of the blanket top referring to Figures 3 and 4.

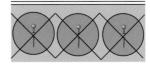

Figure 3

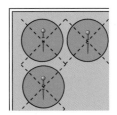

Figure 4

8. Machine-stitch along marked lines through all layers.

9. Turn one fleece circle inside-out by inserting the outside edges through the slits. Adjust the slit edges to form a square (Figures 5 and 6).

10. Pinch raised fleece to form an X shape. Center and pin a motif on a stitched circle, and machine-stitch in place (Figure 7). Repeat with remaining motifs. ●

Figure 5

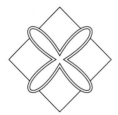

Figure 6

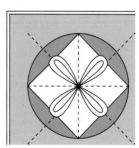

Figure 7

Sailboats

Materials

- Fleece for blanket top and backing*
- ⅛ yard fleece for boats and sails*
- Rotary cutter with scallop blade
- Basic sewing supplies and equipment

Sample was made with blue fleece for top and backing, red fleece for boats and white fleece for sails.

Assembly

Refer to the General Instructions as needed for preparing templates, cutting fleece to size and other construction methods.

1. With wrong sides together, center the blanket top on the backing and pin around the edges through both layers. Hand-stitch ¾ inch from the edge using a running stitch.

2. Using a rotary cutter with a scallop blade, trim around the edges.

3. To determine the number of sailboats that you will need, measure the outside edges of your blanket and divide by 5. This will give you an approximate number of sailboats needed. Sailboats can be adjusted for even spacing before stitching in place.

4. Prepare templates for the boat and sail pieces using patterns on page 64. Cut the desired number of each as determined in step 3.

5. Fold the sails in half but do not match corners as shown in Figure 1; pin.

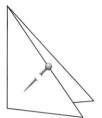

Figure 1

6. Starting in the center of one edge and working toward the corners, pin the boats ½ inch from the seam. Adjust spacing as necessary. Insert two pins in each shape (Figure 2).

Figure 2

7. Pin folded sails in place leaving ½ inch between boats and sails (Figure 3).

Figure 3

8. Mark the stitching lines for the masts ⅛ inch right of the sail folds. Carefully unfold each sail and pin in place. Extend the marked lines onto the bottom edges of the sails ½ inch (Figure 4).

Figure 4

9. Remove the top pins in one boat piece and fold down. With a narrow satin stitch, machine zigzag-stitch along the marked mast line starting inside the sail piece to below the top edge of the boat (Figure 5).

Figure 5

10. Re-pin boats in place. Refold and pin sails in place.

11. Repeat steps 9 and 10 with the remaining boats.

12. Machine-stitch along the curved edge of each boat (Figure 6). Machine-stitch along the angled edges of each sail (Figure 7). ●

Figure 6

Figure 7

Double Dutch

Materials

- Fleece for blanket top*
- Contrasting fleece for blanket backing*
- 2 colors contrasting yarn
- Basic sewing supplies and equipment

Sample was made with medium blue fleece for top, light blue fleece for backing, and light blue and orange yarn for weaving.

Assembly

Refer to the General Instructions as needed for construction methods and cutting fleece to size.

1. Mark a line 2¼ inches from edges of the blanket top.

2. With wrong sides together, center the blanket top on the backing and pin along the marked line through both layers. Machine-stitch along the marked line.

3. Starting 2¼ inches in from the corners, cut ½-inch-wide perpendicular slits in the blanket top only, to within ⅛ inch of the stitched seam (Figure 1). Cut out squares at seam corners (Figure 2).

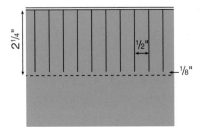

Figure 1

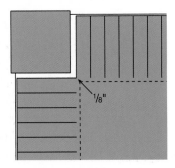

Figure 2

4. Making sure to keep strips flat with edges together, machine-stitch a seam ½ inch from the first stitched seam; repeat to make a third stitched seam ½ inch from the second seam (Figure 3).

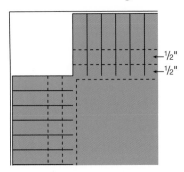

Figure 3

5. Thread a tapestry needle with a 24–28-inch length of one color of yarn. Working right to left, insert the needle under the first strip in the top channel, and draw it back up leaving a 4" tail. Repeat with the needle in the same insertion point and slide it under two strips. Draw it back up and pull the yarn slightly to cinch the strip (Figure 4).

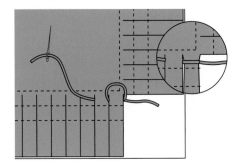

Figure 4

6. Repeat step 5 to wrap each strip (Figure 5). When it becomes necessary to attach a new yarn length, tie ends together, trim ends and adjust the knot to hide under a strip. Leave a 4-inch length of yarn at opposite end.

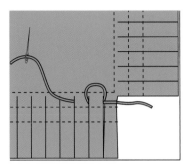

Figure 5

7. Repeat steps 5 and 6 with the second color of yarn in the outside channel (Figure 6).

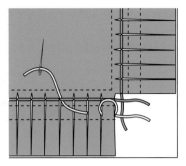

Figure 6

8. Repeat steps 4–7 on each side.

9. Tie knots at each corner with the 4-inch trimmed ends (Figure 7). ●

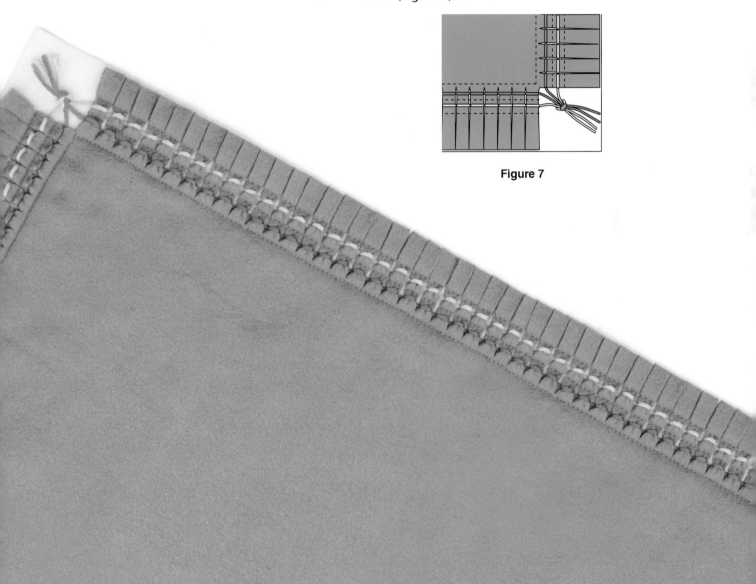

Figure 7

English Garden Quilt

Materials

- Fleece for blanket top*
- Contrasting fleece for blanket backing*
- Water-soluble stabilizer*
- Light and dark shades of thread*
- Basic sewing supplies and equipment

*Sample was made with light green fleece for blanket top, cream fleece for backing, Solvy™ water-soluble stabilizer from Sulky®, dark purple and tan thread.

Assembly

1. Trim ½ inch from the top edge and one side edge of the blanket top. With wrong sides together, center the blanket top on the backing.

2. Cut 5-inch-wide strips of stabilizer. With a water-soluble marking pen, trace the lines of the stitching pattern on page 61 on the stabilizer. Adjust design as needed to meet at the center of blanket sides. Place the stabilizer on the blanket top and pin through all layers.

3. Machine-stitch along the marked lines.

4. Cut away large sections of stabilizer, then immerse the blanket sides in water to remove any remaining stabilizer. Let dry. ●

Fringe Fling

Materials

- Fleece for blanket top*
- Contrasting fleece for blanket backing*
- Chenille yarn
- Basic sewing supplies and equipment

Sample was made with red fleece for top, pink fleece for backing and white chenille yarn.

Project Note: *Finished size of blanket will determine the required yardage of chenille yarn needed. Measure the entire length of the marked line in step 1 and add 2".*

Assembly

Refer to the General Instructions as needed for construction methods and cutting fleece to size.

1. Trim ¼ inch around outside edge of blanket top. Mark a line 1¾ inches from the edge.

2. With wrong sides together, center the blanket top on the backing and pin along marked line through both layers.

3. Place the chenille yarn on the marked line and, with a three-step zigzag stitch, machine-stitch along the yarn (Figure 1).

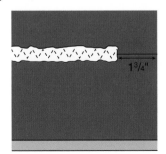

Figure 1

4. Overlap ends slightly and trim to finish ends (Figure 2).

Figure 2   **Figure 3**

5. Fold the blanket-top edge in toward the center of the blanket along the yarn stitching line and pin to secure out of the way (Figure 3).

6. Cut perpendicular slits in the backing from the edge to the seam. Cut slits approximately ⅜ inch wide. Trim squares from corners (Figure 4).

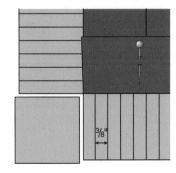

Figure 4

7. Remove pins and carefully cut ⅜-inch slits in the blanket top from the edge to the seam. Trim squares from corners as in step 6. ●

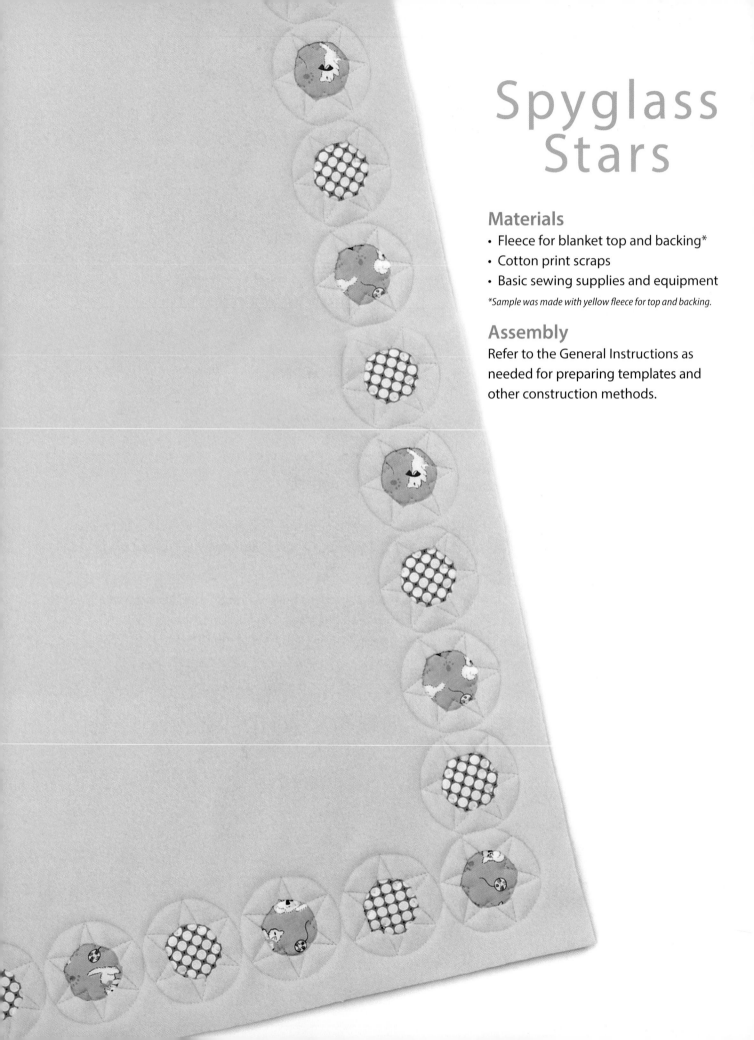

Spyglass Stars

Materials
- Fleece for blanket top and backing*
- Cotton print scraps
- Basic sewing supplies and equipment

Sample was made with yellow fleece for top and backing.

Assembly
Refer to the General Instructions as needed for preparing templates and other construction methods.

1. Prepare templates for the large circle, medium circle, small circle and star shapes using patterns on page 63. Make enough large circle templates to complete one side of blanket.

2. Mark a line on the blanket top ¾ inch from outside edge.

3. Align one large circle at each of two adjoining corners and pin in place (Figure 1). Continue placing and pinning circles along the marked line. Adjust the circles for even spacing and trace around each template. Repeat with the remaining three sides.

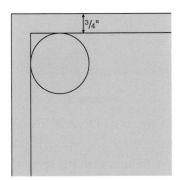

Figure 1

4. With wrong sides together, center the blanket top on the backing and pin around edges through both layers. Machine-stitch around marked circles.

5. Center and trace one small circle inside each large circle (Figure 2).

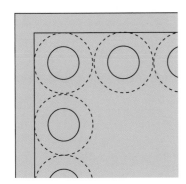

Figure 2

6. Cutting through the blanket top layer only, carefully cut along the marked lines of the small circles (Figure 3).

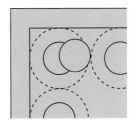

Figure 3

7. Cut medium circles from scrap fabrics.

8. Carefully insert and center one medium circle inside one small circle opening (Figure 4). Do not stretch the cut edge of the small circle.

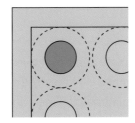

Figure 4

9. Center the star template on the circle and mark around the edge. Machine-stitch along the marked lines to complete one circle cutout motif (Figure 5).

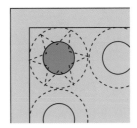

Figure 5

10. Repeat steps 8 and 9 with the remaining circles. ●

Stuffed Clouds

Materials
- Fleece for blanket top and backing*
- Fiberfill
- Basic sewing supplies and equipment

Sample was made with blue fleece for top and backing.

Assembly

Refer to the General Instructions as needed for preparing template, cutting fleece to size and other construction methods.

1. Prepare the cloud template using the pattern on page 64. Make enough templates to complete one side of blanket.

2. Align one template at each of two adjoining corners and pin in place (Figure 1). Continue placing and pinning templates along the edge. Adjust the templates for even spacing and trace around each. Repeat with the remaining three sides.

Figure 1

3. With wrong sides together, center the blanket top on the backing and pin around edges through both layers.

4. Machine-stitch around three sides of one cloud shape, securing stitches at the beginning and end of each seam and leaving the outer side open (Figure 2). Repeat with the remaining shapes.

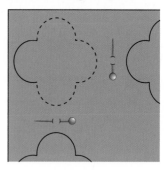

Figure 2

5. Stuff a small amount of fiberfill in one stitched cloud shape through the opening (Figure 3). Pin the opening closed. Repeat with the remaining shapes.

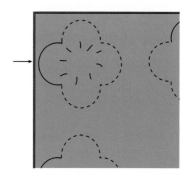

Figure 3

6. Machine-stitch the opening edges closed on each cloud shape.

7. Carefully trim around the outer half of each cloud shape to within ¼ inch of the seams, and horizontally between shapes (Figure 4). ●

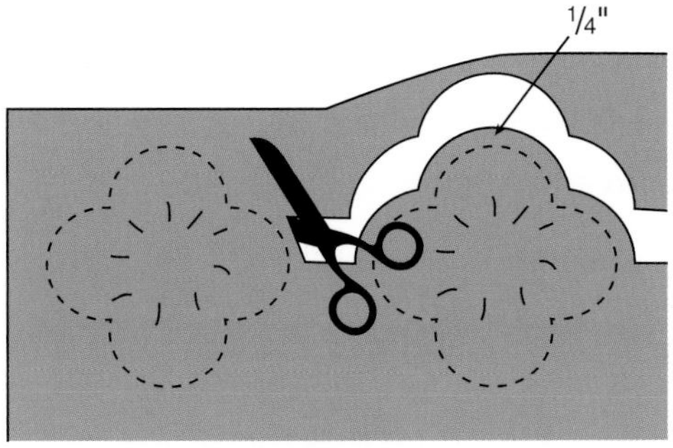

Figure 4

Origami

Materials

- Fleece for blanket top*
- Fleece, flannel or lightweight cotton jersey for blanket backing*
- Cotton flannel long enough to cut border strips for the longest sides along the length of fabric
- Basic sewing supplies and equipment

Sample was made with white-with-blue print fleece for top, white cotton jersey for backing and melon cotton flannel for edging.

Project Notes: *Preshrink the cotton flannel for trim and the cotton jersey if using for backing fabric.*

Lengthwise strips of flannel are used to avoid having to seam strips together to make the required lengths to avoid seams in loops.

Assembly

Refer to the General Instructions as needed for construction methods.

1. Determine desired blanket size and subtract 1 inch from both the width and length. Cut one piece of fleece for blanket top and one piece of backing fabric. With wrong sides together, center the blanket top on the backing and pin around edges through both layers. Baste layers together ¼ inch from edges.

2. Cut four 5¼-inch-wide border strips of cotton flannel along the length of fabric to correspond to the length of the blanket sides. Trim two of these strips to correspond to the width of the top and bottom of the blanket.

3. With right sides together and using a ½-inch seam allowance, stitch a long border strip to opposite sides of the blanket top starting and stopping stitching ½ inch from the top and bottom edges of the blanket top. Trim ½ inch from each end of each strip as shown in Figure 1.

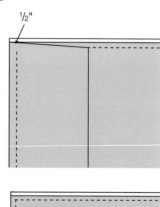

Figure 1

4. Fold the long raw edge of each strip over the seam allowance to the back side of the blanket leaving 2⅛ inches on the front side and 2⅝ inches on the back side (Figure 2); pin the raw edges on the back along stitched seams (Figure 3).

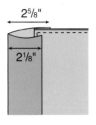
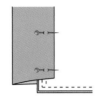

Figure 2   **Figure 3**

5. Machine-stitch next to the fold on the top side of border strips through all layers (Figure 4).

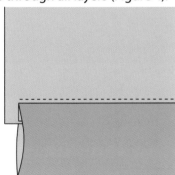

Figure 4

6. With remaining border strips, repeat steps 3–5 on the top and bottom, except start and stop seams at blanket edges.

7. Make perpendicular cuts in flannel border to within ¼ inch of the seam on the blanket top (Figure 5).

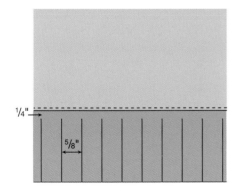

Figure 5

8. Place the blanket on a flat work surface with the wrong side up. Working from right to left, fold the first loop at a 90-degree angle to the left and insert the adjoining loop inside (Figures 6, 7 and 8).

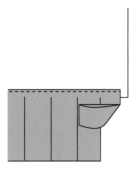

Figure 6

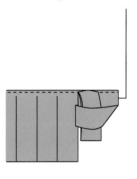

Figure 7

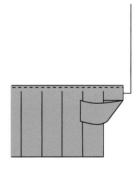

Figure 8

9. Repeat step 8 along each side. Fold last loop to blanket back and hand-stitch in place to secure. ●

Pattern Templates

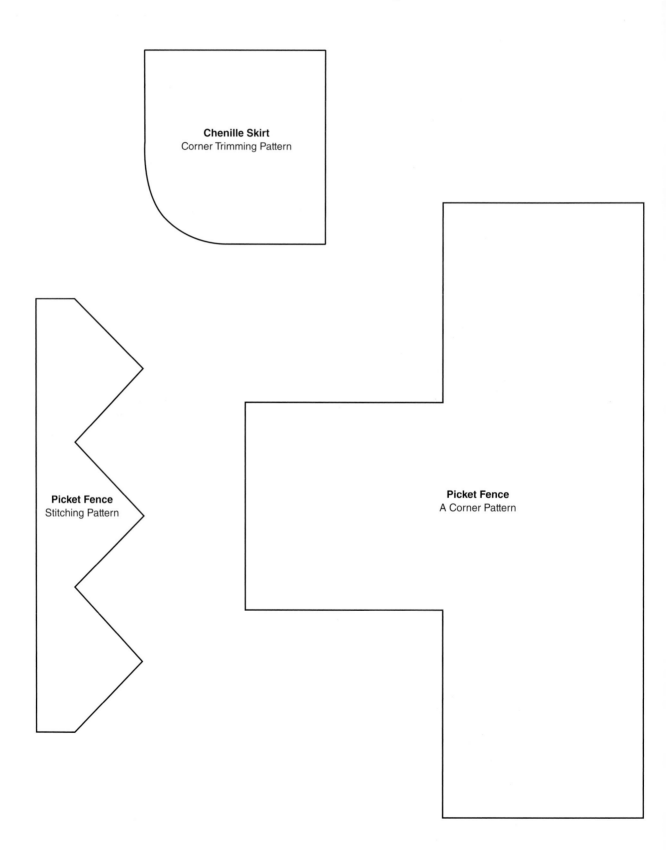

Chenille Skirt
Corner Trimming Pattern

Picket Fence
Stitching Pattern

Picket Fence
A Corner Pattern

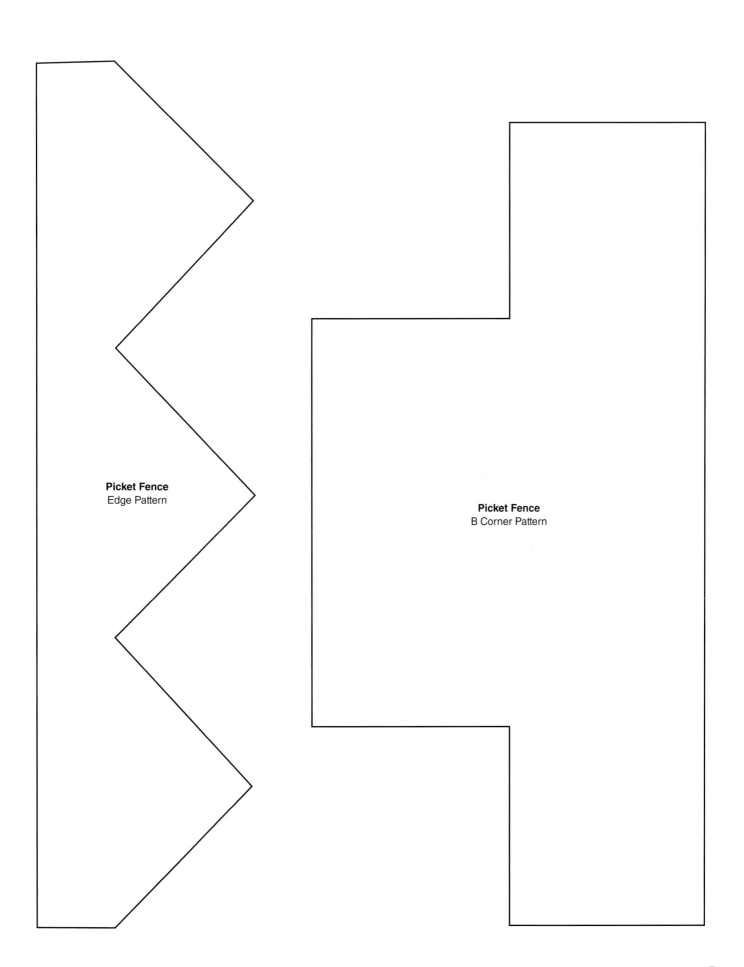

Picket Fence
Edge Pattern

Picket Fence
B Corner Pattern

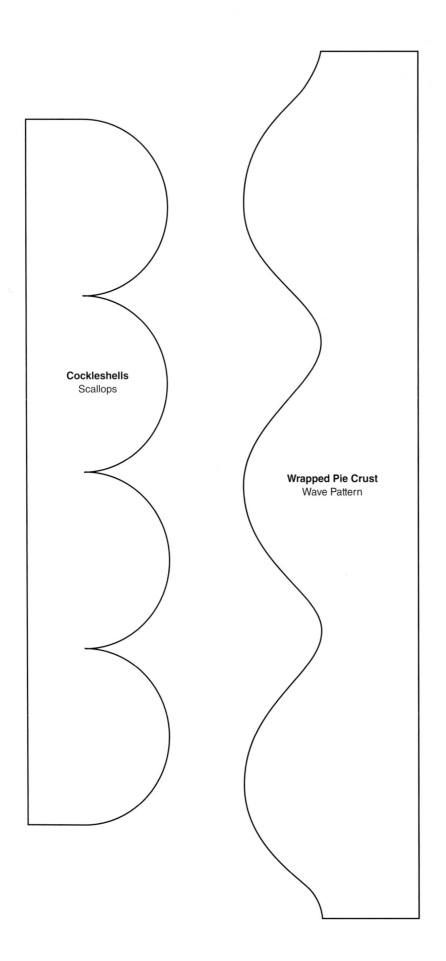

Cockleshells
Scallops

Wrapped Pie Crust
Wave Pattern

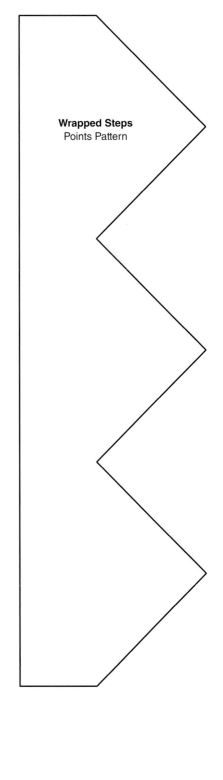

Wrapped Steps
Points Pattern

English Garden Quilt
Stitching Pattern

Jersey Chain
Chain Pattern

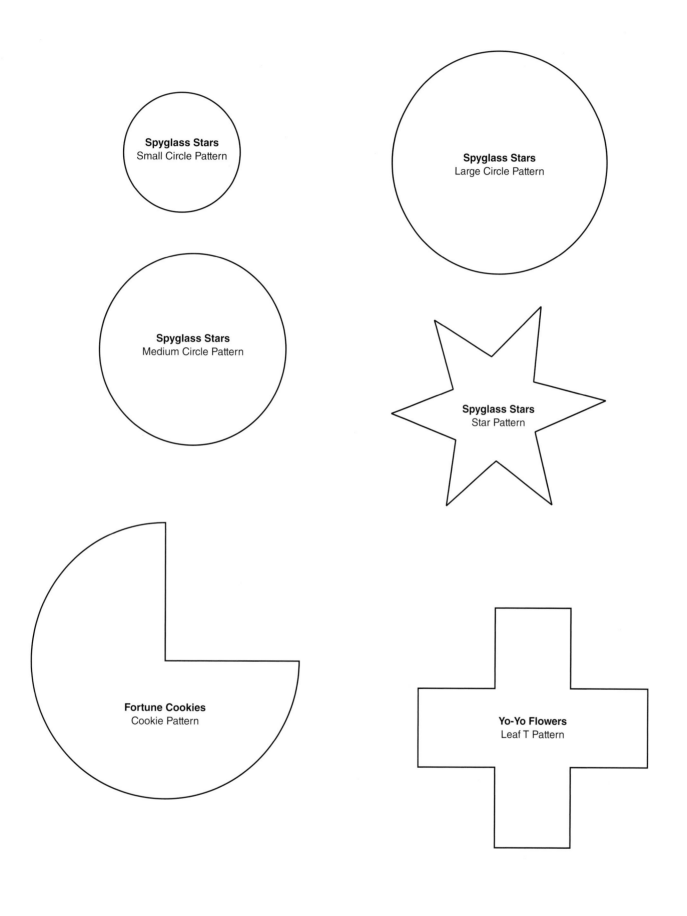

Spyglass Stars
Small Circle Pattern

Spyglass Stars
Large Circle Pattern

Spyglass Stars
Medium Circle Pattern

Spyglass Stars
Star Pattern

Fortune Cookies
Cookie Pattern

Yo-Yo Flowers
Leaf T Pattern

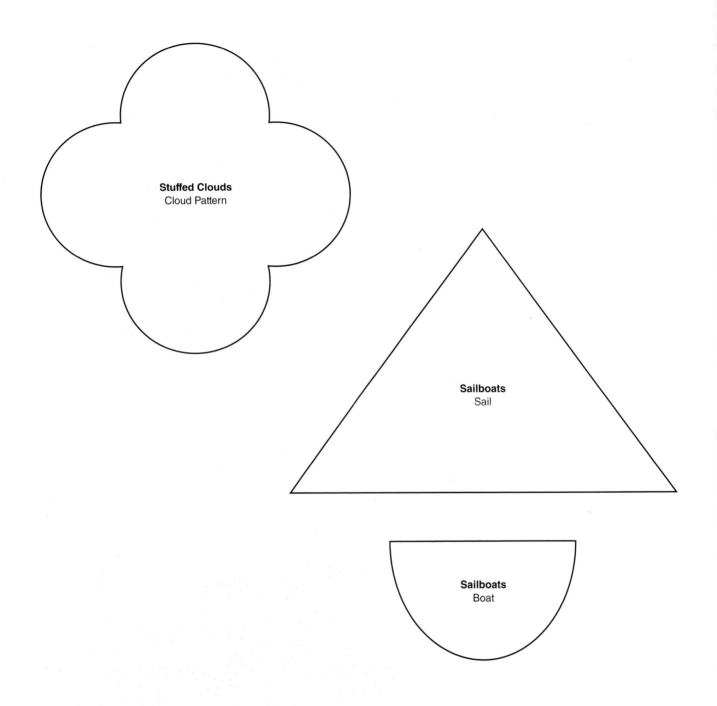

Stuffed Clouds
Cloud Pattern

Sailboats
Sail

Sailboats
Boat

ISBN: 978-1-57367-694-6

1 2 3 4 5 6 7 8 9